MW01064189

It's My State! ★ ★ ★ ★ ★

OKLAHOMA

The Sooner State

Gerry Boehme, Geoffrey M. Horn, and Doug Sanders

Cavendish Square

New York

Published in 2016 by Cavendish Square Publishing, LLC
243 5th Avenue, Suite 136, New York, NY 10016

Third Edition

Website: cavendishsq.com

This publication represents the opinions and views of the author based on his or her personal experience, knowledge, and research. The information in this book serves as a general guide only. The author and publisher have used their best efforts in preparing this book and disclaim liability rising directly or indirectly from the use and application of this book.

CPSIA Compliance Information: Batch #WS15CSQ

All websites were available and accurate when this book was sent to press.

Library of Congress Cataloging-in-Publication Data

Boehme, Gerry.
Oklahoma / Gerry Boehme, Doug Sanders, and Geoffrey Horn.
pages cm. — (It's my state!)
Includes bibliographical references and index.
ISBN 978-1-62713-213-8 (hardcover) ISBN 978-1-62713-215-2 (ebook)
1. Oklahoma—Juvenile literature. I. Sanders, Doug, 1972- II. Horn, Geoffrey M. III. Title.

F694.3.B64 2016
976.6—dc23

2014049516

Editorial Director: David McNamara
Editor: Fletcher Doyle
Copy Editor: Rebecca Rohan
Art Director: Jeffrey Talbot
Designer: Stephanie Flecha
Senior Production Manager: Jennifer Ryder-Talbot
Production Editor: Renni Johnson
Photo Research by J8 Media

Printed in the United States of America

OKLAHOMA ★ ★ ★

CONTENTS

A QUICK LOOK AT
STATEHOOD: NOVEMBER 16, 1907

State Animal: Bison

Long before Oklahoma became a state, millions of bison (also known as buffalo) roamed the Great Plains. By the 1890s, fewer than one thousand remained and concerned citizens began to protect this important American animal. Today, bison can be found in Oklahoma parks and wildlife sanctuaries, and on the plains.

animals and plants in Oklahoma!

[Scissor]-Tailed Flycatcher

[...] the bobwhite as the state [...] instead chose the flycatcher [...] its extremely long, black- [...] the elaborate "sky dance" it

State Butterfly: Black Swallowtail

As a caterpillar, this insect sports a vibrant pattern of white, black, and green stripes with rows of yellow dots. As a butterfly, the swallowtail is mostly black with bands or spots of yellow. Adults draw the nectar from red clover, milkweed, and thistle.

OKLAHOMA
POPULATION: 3,751,351

★ State Floral Emblem: Mistletoe

Although mistletoe is not really a flower, it became
an official territorial symbol in 1893. Mistletoe lives on
trees that grow across the state. The dark green leaves
and white berries of the plant are a common sight in
Oklahoma in fall and winter.

★ State Reptile: Collared Lizard

Oklahoma's collared lizards can frequently be seen
sunning themselves in the Wichita Mountains. Early white
settlers nicknamed this silent reptile "mountain boomer,"
because they believed it made the loud noises they were
hearing. The settlers were probably hearing the loud calls
of frogs.

★ State Tree: Redbud

In spring, the redbud's clusters of pinkish flowers
often bloom before the heart-shaped leaves appear.
The redbud became the official tree in 1937, prompting
one poet to write: "And this is Oklahoma's tree of
loveliness so rare, / A symbol of red earth and free,
when blooming anywhere."

The Milky Way provides a glowing backdrop for the Wedding Rock formation in the Black Mesa area.

1

The Sooner State

Oklahoma's land is as varied as its people. The state, which covers seventy-seven counties, mostly consists of a massive rolling plain. It slopes gently downward as it unfolds from northwest to southeast. Those two compass points mark the two extremes of the state's geography and climate.

The state's highest point is Black **Mesa**, near the border with New Mexico and Colorado. At 4,973 feet (1,516 meters), Oklahoma's highest point offers great views of the surrounding area. The mesa—which is a small, isolated hill with steep sides—is located at the northwest tip of the Oklahoma Panhandle. The Panhandle is a strip of land 166 miles (267 kilometers) long and 34 miles (55 km) wide. As its name suggests, it looks like a handle that is sticking out of the state's northwestern corner.

Oklahoma's lowest point in elevation is found in the southeast, at the opposite corner of the state. Near Idabel, close to the border with Texas and Arkansas, the land dips to 289 feet (88 m) above sea level.

OKLAHOMA
COUNTY MAP

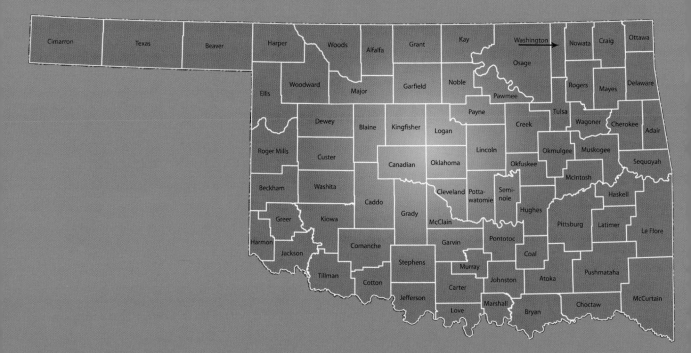

Cimarron · Texas · Beaver · Harper · Woods · Alfalfa · Grant · Kay · Washington · Nowata · Craig · Ottawa · Osage · Ellis · Woodward · Major · Garfield · Noble · Rogers · Mayes · Delaware · Pawnee · Tulsa · Dewey · Blaine · Kingfisher · Payne · Creek · Wagoner · Cherokee · Adair · Roger Mills · Logan · Lincoln · Okmulgee · Muskogee · Sequoyah · Custer · Canadian · Oklahoma · Okfuskee · McIntosh · Beckham · Washita · Cleveland · Potta-watomie · Semi-nole · Haskell · Caddo · Hughes · Pittsburg · Latimer · Le Flore · Greer · Kiowa · Grady · McClain · Pontotoc · Coal · Harmon · Comanche · Garvin · Atoka · Pushmataha · Jackson · Tillman · Murray · Johnston · Stephens · Cotton · Carter · McCurtain · Jefferson · Love · Marshall · Bryan · Choctaw

County	Population	County	Population	County	Population
Adair	22,683	Greer	6,239	Oklahoma	718,633
Alfalfa	5,642	Harmon	2,922	Okmulgee	40,069
Atoka	14,182	Harper	3,685	Osage	47,472
Beaver	5,636	Haskell	12,769	Ottawa	31,848
Beckham	22,119	Hughes	14,003	Pawnee	16,577
Blaine	11,943	Jackson	26,446	Payne	77,350
Bryan	42,416	Jefferson	6,472	Pittsburg	45,837
Caddo	29,600	Johnston	10,957	Pontotoc	37,492
Canadian	115,541	Kay	46,562	Pottawatomie	69,442
Carter	47,557	Kingfisher	15,034	Pushmataha	11,572
Cherokee	46,987	Kiowa	9,446	Roger Mills	3,647
Choctaw	15,205	Latimer	11,154	Rogers	86,905
Cimarron	2,475	Le Flore	50,384	Seminole	25,482
Cleveland	255,755	Lincoln	34,273	Sequoyah	42,391
Coal	5,925	Logan	41,848	Stephens	45,048
Comanche	124,098	Love	9,423	Texas	20,640
Cotton	6,193	McClain	34,506	Tillman	7,992
Craig	15,029	McCurtain	33,151	Tulsa	603,403
Creek	69,967	McIntosh	20,252	Wagoner	73,085
Custer	27,469	Major	7,527	Washington	50,976
Delaware	41,487	Marshall	15,840	Washita	11,629
Dewey	4,810	Mayes	41,259	Woods	8,878
Ellis	4,151	Murray	13,488	Woodward	20,081
Garfield	60,580	Muskogee	70,990		
Garvin	27,576	Noble	11,561		
Grady	52,431	Nowata	10,536		
Grant	4,527	Okfuskee	12,191		

Source: US Bureau of the Census, 2010

The Ouachita National Forest provides hiking and camping opportunities in Oklahoma's Green Country.

Eastern Oklahoma

Eastern Oklahoma is a region of flat, fertile plains and low hills. One of the most notable features is the Ozark Plateau. A plateau is a stretch of raised land with a nearly level surface. The Ozark Plateau extends into the state from nearby Missouri and Arkansas. Residents often refer to this part of the state as Oklahoma's Green Country. Clear, swift-flowing rivers and streams help keep the area lush. The waters flow through steep-walled valleys, which break up the wide stretches of flat-topped uplands. The rivers helped create these valleys and the high bluffs that often line the banks. Over millions of years, the water's flow slowly carved these trenches into the land.

The southeastern part of Oklahoma is heavily forested and supports an active lumber industry. The region is also home to the Ouachitas, one of the state's few mountain chains. The Ouachitas consist of groups of tall sandstone ridges that stretch from west to east. The Ouachitas make up one of the most rugged regions in the state. Natural springs bubble up, and sparkling streams course in and out of the many valleys tucked between the ridges.

Oklahoma Borders

North:	Colorado
	Kansas
South:	Texas
East:	Arkansas
	Missouri
West:	Texas
	New Mexico

Between the Ozark Plateau and the Ouachitas is the region known as the Prairie Plains. Crops thrive in this part of Oklahoma, which is flat and mostly treeless. East of Muskogee, the Arkansas River Valley is an especially fertile part of the state. Much of the state's coal and major pockets of petroleum are also found there.

Central Oklahoma

Like the eastern region, Central Oklahoma features a variety of landscapes. Starting on the northern edge of the state, near the border with Kansas, sandstone hills rise 250 to 400 feet (75 to 120 m) high. Many of the hills are lined with flowering blackjack plants and with post oaks and other types of trees. The sandstone hills run almost the entire length of the state. This region includes Oklahoma's second-largest city, Tulsa.

In the south, the plains eventually give way to the rolling Red River region. This area of the state, along the Texas border, was important to Oklahoma's early petroleum industry, and major oil fields are still found there. The Red River region extends all the way to the state's southeastern corner, where it meets up with the Ouachitas. This fertile area is known for its rolling prairie and forests. The sandy soil is among the state's richest. Vegetables are a common sight growing in the fields.

The Red Bed Plains are found to the west of the sandstone hills. They form the largest land region in the state. Included in this region is the state capital, Oklahoma City. Like the sandstone hills, this area stretches from the Kansas border to southern Oklahoma's boundary with Texas. As the Red Bed Plains gently slope upward to the west, a few forests give way to grasslands. The land supports some farming and livestock herding.

The Arkansas River runs past Oklahoma's second largest city, Tulsa.

Turner Falls is the largest waterfall in Oklahoma, dropping 77 feet (23 m).

The soil is made up of a combination of materials, mostly clay mixed with harder layers of sandstone and **gypsum**. The region is crossed by several streams, which flow from the High Plains located to the northwest.

The low-rising Arbuckle Mountains add to the variety of Central Oklahoma landforms. The Arbuckles rise from about 700 feet (215 m) above sea level in the east to 1,400 feet (425 m) in the west and cover about 1,000 square miles (2,600 sq km) in the south-central part of the state. They are an ancient mountain system. Granite found in Johnston County, just north of the Texas border, is about 1.4 billion years old. The portion of the Arbuckles in this area is the oldest exposed rock between the southern Appalachians to the east and the Rocky Mountains to the west.

The Chickasaw National Recreation Area, Turner Falls, Price Falls, and the Arbuckle Wilderness Park are some of the natural attractions found in this part of the state. The Arbuckles also contain commercially valuable minerals, such as iron ore, lead, zinc, limestone, and granite.

Western Oklahoma

Oklahoma's portion of the Great Plains is found in the west. This elevated region consists mostly of thick grasslands. It is also home to wheat fields and the grazing lands that fatten much of the state's livestock. This area is sometimes called the High Plains. This portion of Oklahoma is but a small part of the immense grasslands that extend northward from central Texas all the way up into Canada.

The grasslands rise gently from about 2,000 feet (610 m) in the region's eastern edge to almost 5,000 feet (1,525 m) at the western end of the Panhandle. The flat surface of the High Plains is broken only by large streams and circular features often called sinks or playa lakes, which fill with water after spring rains but may be dry at other times of the year. These small bodies of water are scattered across the plains and help support the area's wildlife.

Like the rest of the state, Western Oklahoma offers its share of surprises. Sudden outcroppings of sandstone and gypsum, sharp ravines, and stark hills leave their mark on the northwest and the Panhandle. The southwest is also home to one of the state's most impressive mountain chains, the Wichitas. These granite peaks are about 525 million years old.

The Wichitas range from 400 to 1,100 feet (125 to 335 m), though some peaks reach above 2,400 feet (735 m). At 2,464 feet (751m), Mount Scott is perhaps the best-known peak in the range. Its summit, or highest point, can be reached on foot or by car or bus. The view from Mount Scott reveals some of the state's most stunning scenery, including a great view of the region's many human-made lakes, or **reservoirs**. These lakes were created by damming the many streams that flow out of the range. The area has become a valuable source of granite, limestone, and sand and gravel. Smaller amounts of gold, silver, copper, lead, zinc, aluminum, and iron ores are also found in the Wichitas.

The Gypsum Hills are another important part of Western Oklahoma. They lie west of the Red Bed Plains and eventually meet the High Plains in the northwestern portion

Playa lakes are filled by the rain in spring.

★10 KEY SITES★ ★

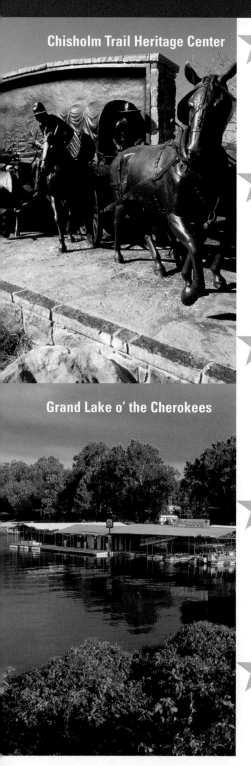

Chisholm Trail Heritage Center

Grand Lake o' the Cherokees

1. Black Mesa State Park and Nature Reserve

Located in the state's northwest corner, the Black Mesa plateau is Oklahoma's highest point at 4,973 feet (1,516 m). Nearby, Black Mesa State Park and Nature Preserve features amazing wildlife including golden eagles and bighorn sheep.

2. Bricktown

The area now known as Bricktown is located in downtown Oklahoma City. Founded just after the Land Run of 1889, Bricktown once served as a central hub of the state. It is now a thriving entertainment district filled with museums, attractions, and restaurants.

3. Chisholm Trail Heritage Center

Located on the historic Chisholm Trail in Duncan, Oklahoma, the Chisholm Trail Heritage Center offers an interactive Old West experience. Smell prairie wildflowers, listen to the thundering hooves of a cattle stampede, and feel wind and rain on your face.

4. Glover River

Oklahoma's last major free-flowing river without dams or water releases, the Glover River offers secluded beauty, canoeing, and bass fishing. The fact that the river is still un-commercialized lures the most experienced adventurer to southeast Oklahoma.

5. Grand Lake o' the Cherokees

Grand Lake o' the Cherokees is one of Oklahoma's most popular lake destinations. It has 1,300 miles (2,092 km) of scenic shoreline bordered by five state parks.

6. National Cowboy & Western Heritage Museum

The National Cowboy Western & Heritage Museum is America's premier institution of Western history, art, and culture. This Oklahoma City Museum collects, preserves, and exhibits a collection of Western art and **artifacts**.

7. Oklahoma City National Memorial

This beautiful museum was built to honor those who were killed during the Oklahoma City bombing on April 19, 1995. The story is told in chapters and takes visitors through the event, ending with a message of hope for today.

8. The Spiro Mounds Archaeological Center

The Spiro Mounds are one of the most important prehistoric Native American archaeological sites in the nation. The Spiro Mounds were created and used by Native Americans between 850 and 1450 CE.

9. The Talimena National Scenic Byway

This breathtaking, 54-mile (87 km) route in southeast Oklahoma was built to highlight the area's beautiful foliage. It is designated as an official National Scenic Byway and spans one of the highest mountain ranges between the Appalachians and the Rockies.

10. Wichita Mountains Wildlife Refuge

The Wichita Mountains Wildlife Refuge was established to protect animals in grave danger of extinction, and to restore species that had been eliminated from the area. The refuge includes bison, elk, wild turkeys, prairie dogs, river otters, and burrowing owls.

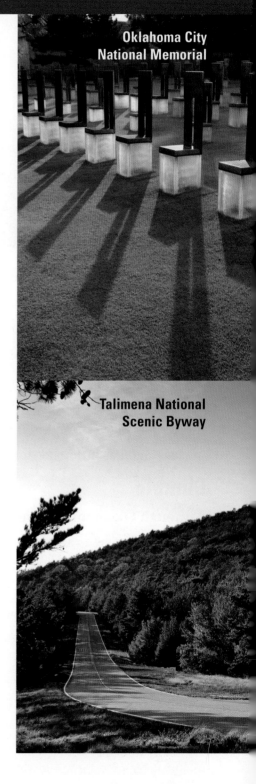

Oklahoma City National Memorial

Talimena National Scenic Byway

Summer winds can fan the flames of wildfires in the grasslands.

of the state. These hills range in height from 150 to 200 feet (45 to 60 m). Each of the hills is capped with a layer of gypsum 15 to 20 feet (5 to 6 m) thick. The gypsum is mined to make plaster and other products. From a distance, the Gypsum Hills seem to sparkle in the sunlight. Because of that unique feature, they are sometimes called the Glass Hills.

At first glance, Western Oklahoma appears to be a dry, almost desert-like region. But the area receives enough rainfall to be blanketed with a variety of wildflowers and prairie grasses, such as little bluestem and hairy grama. Red cedars also dot the landscape.

Climate

Although Oklahoma is generally known for its warm, dry climate, state residents experience a wide range of weather. The northwest tends to be cooler and a bit drier than areas in the southeast. In winter months, temperature regularly drop below 0 degrees Fahrenheit (−18 degrees Celsius). North winds often descend on the Great Plains with their icy blasts.

In summer, the sun beats down on the treeless grasslands, and few things stir during the height of the midday heat. Temperatures can often rise well above 100°F (38°C). Hot, dry, and windy conditions can lead to prairie fires and **tornadoes**.

In Their Own Words

"If you don't like the weather in Oklahoma, wait a minute and it'll change."
–Will Rogers

Precipitation, the amount of moisture the state receives, can vary greatly throughout the state. The southeast averages about 56 inches (142 centimeters) of rain per year. Conditions are very different in the Panhandle, which receives an average of 17 inches (43 cm) of rain annually. Snowstorms are rare in the southeast, dropping an annual average of only 2 inches (5 cm) on the region. People living in the Panhandle, though, have to shovel their way through up to 30 inches (76 cm) of snow per year.

Oklahoma Wildlife

Oklahoma's diverse terrain is home to a wide range of plants and animals. Oak, hickory, elm, pine, and ash are some of the trees that make up the woodlands of Eastern Oklahoma. White-tailed deer, raccoons, foxes, squirrels, and opossums make their homes in and among the trees.

As a prairie state, Oklahoma is also known for its wild grasses. These grasses help to feed the state's livestock and have colorful names such as bluestem, hairy grama, wiregrass, and sandgrass. Grasses are not the only plants on the prairie. Sagebrush, mesquite, goldenrod, sunflowers, and black-eyed Susans are just a few of the other hearty plants that thrive on the plains. Black-tailed jackrabbits, pocket gophers, and kit foxes roam through the thick grass.

With so many reservoirs and natural lakes, the state is a sport-fishing paradise. Oklahoma is known as bass country, but other species, or types, of fish also are abundant.

A kit fox roams and hunts in the grasslands of Oklahoma.

Prairie dogs must keep a constant watch for predators.

Sunfish, crappies, catfish, and carp gather near the shores or swim along the bottoms of the state's waterways.

Many bird species inhabit the Sooner State. Often, large flocks blot the sky, or a single bird can be seen soaring—the only thing moving above the plains. Meadowlarks perch on fence posts, tilt back their heads, and fill the air with song. Blue jays, cardinals, doves, crows, and mockingbirds gather as well.

The Gypsum Hills are a great place to see the range of plants and animals the state has to offer. Bobcats and coyotes pad about the underbrush in search of a meal. Black-tailed prairie dogs keep a constant watch near their underground dens. They scurry down their holes at the first sign of danger. Armadillos, deer, and roadrunners are common sights as well. Collared lizards, western rattlesnakes, and tarantulas can be found in the shade, hiding from the hot rays of the midday sun.

Under many bridges and outcroppings in the Gypsum Hills, colonies of cliff swallows build their hanging nests out of mud. Fruit from the area's many red cedars attracts winged visitors from far away. During the winter, flocks of mountain bluebirds descend on the region, hundreds of miles from where they usually make their homes. They feed in the cedars, which also draw a number of birds that have headed south for the winter. Robins, cedar waxwings, and Townsend's solitaires can also be seen flitting among the trees.

Protecting the Environment

Over time some of Oklahoma's plants and animals have become endangered or threatened. Endangered species are plants and animals that are now so rare they may soon become extinct (that is, completely die out). Threatened species are plants and animals that are likely to become endangered soon if nothing is done to preserve them. Some concerned Oklahomans are working to prevent species from becoming threatened or endangered. They help ailing plant and animal communities recover and increase their numbers in the state before it is too late.

Conservation efforts require cooperation. Almost 95 percent of the state's land is privately owned. When there are problems, owners must agree to let wildlife officials step in and offer a solution. The Partners for Fish and Wildlife Program links the federal government, the states, and private landowners in conservation activities. In 1990, Oklahoma began participating in this program, which works to restore land and improve animal populations on privately owned lands across the state.

At first, the program targeted wetlands. Later, wildlife officials focused on improving other areas where threatened and endangered plants and animals live. So far, more than nine hundred projects have been started, affecting practically every Oklahoma county. More than 300,000 acres (120,000 hectares) of wildlife habitat have been restored, including more than 22,000 acres (9,000 ha) of prairie wetlands. These valuable areas support migrating birds and a range of local species.

Conservation workers and concerned citizens know that it takes more than just projects to protect the environment. They believe education is important to ensuring the future of Oklahoma's wildlife. Under the Partners for Fish and Wildlife Program, more than 130 outdoor environmental classrooms have been set up or are being developed in Oklahoma. In these outdoor settings, students can learn about the natural world and what they can do to preserve it. Program officials expect to educate more than two million students in these special outdoor learning centers. Officials hope that these centers will improve students' understanding of how valuable their state's land, animals, and plants really are.

Oklahoma has worked to maintain wildlife habitat.

Armadillo

Grasslands

Indian Blanket

1. Armadillo

Its bony, scaly shell protects the nine-banded armadillo from predators. Armadillos are good diggers and also good swimmers. They eat insects, grubs, and occasionally berries and birds' eggs. When female nine-banded armadillos reproduce, they give birth to four identical babies.

2. Bison

Great herds of bison (also called buffalo) once roamed North America. After most were killed by hunters, efforts began to protect them. The first national preserve for bison was founded in 1907 near Cache, Oklahoma. It later became the Wichita Mountains National Wildlife Reserve.

3. Black Swallowtail Butterfly

Oklahoma is home to a wide variety of colorful butterflies. The black swallowtail is a migratory species and lives in the state from May to October.

4. Grasslands

Grasslands are abundant in Oklahoma. Tallgrasses are found in the northern and eastern sections of the state, most notably at the Tallgrass Prairie Preserve, a 39,000-acre (15,783 ha.) property of the Nature Conservancy with free-ranging buffalo. Grasses in the west are primarily short and mixed.

5. Indian Blanket

Oklahoma's state wildflower, the Indian blanket, usually blooms from June to August and grows 1 to 3 feet (0.3 to 0.9 m) tall. The flower is red in the center with yellow on the tips and thrives in both extreme heat and **drought** conditions.

6. Prairie Rattlesnake

Prairie rattlesnakes coil beneath rocks and can attack if provoked, although their venom is rarely deadly to humans. Living in grasslands in summer and hidden in rocky outcroppings in winter, they feed on small rodents, birds, and other snakes.

7. Red Bat

This nighttime flyer is the only North American bat with different colors for females and males. Females tend to be yellow-brown while males can be a bright orange. Red bats can eat more than a thousand insects per hour.

8. Sandbass

Found in natural lakes and reservoirs across the state, "sandies" are a prize catch. Sandies travel in large schools (groups) and eat other fish—mostly shad—and insects. Most live three or four years, but some live as long as ten years.

9. Texas Horned Lizard

Sometimes confused for toads, horned lizards are named for the unusual hornlike spines on the back of their heads and the smaller spines scattered over their backs and sides. Once common in Oklahoma, they are becoming harder to find.

10. Wild Turkey

The official state game bird, two species of wild turkey live in Oklahoma: the Rio Grande Turkey and the Eastern Wild Turkey. Oklahoma's wild turkeys were almost wiped out by the early 1940s, but effective wildlife management has restored them.

Prairie Rattlesnake

Red Bat

Wild Turkey

This stone effigy pipe, used in religious ceremonies circa 1200 CE, was found at Spiro Mound.

From the Beginning

2

Humans have been living in Oklahoma for more than twelve thousand years. At a site near Anadarko, archaeologists—scientists who study the past—found several spear points and the bones of a mammoth (a large mammal that is now extinct). They have connected these artifacts with a group of people known as the Clovis culture. This ancient group most likely wandered into the region following herds of animals. The plains proved to be an ideal place to search for food. Many prehistoric creatures came to the grasslands to graze and mate. Giant mammoths, musk-oxen, ground sloths, elk, reindeer, bears, and an early version of the horse all made the plains their home.

Eventually these early people of the Clovis culture shifted their focus to one main food source—the bison. Small groups of people would follow the wandering herds for part or most of the year. They also gathered plants, eating whatever they could find. These hunter-gatherers would build temporary shelters, live in them for a brief time, and then move on.

About 2,500 years ago, another shift occurred. People settled into a more stable lifestyle. Farming, mostly of corn and beans, became important.

From 500 to 1300 CE, a group known as the Mound Builders lived in what would become Le Flore County, just west of the Arkansas-Oklahoma border. They built huge earthen mounds to honor their dead. Artifacts found in these burial mounds show that

Many works of art were found at Spiro Mound, including this shell carving that was worn around someone's neck.

the Mound Builders made artwork and many useful objects by hand. They also had a complex economy that involved a large trading network. It stretched from the Great Lakes to the Pacific coast.

By the time Europeans arrived in the region in the sixteenth century, members of the Caddo Nation were living in what is now southeastern Oklahoma. The Quapaw settled in present-day northeastern Oklahoma, where they lived as farmers and hunter-gatherers. The Wichita adopted a similar lifestyle. They built grass houses along rivers and streams in the southern and eastern parts of the area. Later arrivals in the northeast, the Osage, mostly farmed. But their hunting parties made annual bison hunts on the plains to the west.

Other groups of Native Americans, including the Cheyenne, Arapaho, Comanche, and Plains Apache, would also enter what is now Western Oklahoma, following the bison herds. The Kiowa and Pawnee were other major Native American nations in the region, adding to the great variety of tribes living on the plains.

Europeans Arrive

The first European to enter present-day Oklahoma was most likely Francisco Vásquez de Coronado. He crossed the region in 1541, leading an expedition that started in present-day New Mexico. Hernando de Soto, another Spanish explorer, may have passed through what is now Eastern Oklahoma as well. They were both in search of gold but, finding none, soon moved on.

In 1601, Juan de Oñate traveled through the western portion of the present-day state, also in search of gold. His group reached the site of today's city of Wichita, Kansas, then turned around and headed back to the Southwest. Oñate was followed by additional Spanish explorers and by French traders from Louisiana looking for new markets for their goods. A seventeenth-century French explorer, René-Robert Cavelier, Sieur de La Salle, claimed the area for France on his journey down the Mississippi River valley. But the Spanish and French newcomers found little to make them stay in the region at that time. The first European trading post was most likely established at Salina in the early 1800s.

At the beginning of the nineteenth century, France held present-day Oklahoma as part of the Louisiana Territory. In 1803, the US government paid $15 million to buy the entire territory from France. This land sale, known as the Louisiana Purchase, brought what is now Oklahoma under US government control. The purchased territory also included today's states of Arkansas, Missouri, Iowa, Kansas, and Nebraska, as well as parts of Minnesota, North Dakota, South Dakota, New Mexico, Texas, Montana, Wyoming, Colorado, and Louisiana.

Following the Louisiana Purchase, some important white settlements sprang up in the territory of Oklahoma, including Miller Court House, located in today's McCurtain County, and Three Forks in the northeast. But beyond the occasional trader, explorer, or curious traveler, most of the region stayed in the hands of Native Americans.

Because of the area's remote location, the Native Americans' contacts with whites developed slowly. As the Wichita and other Native American nations began trading with outsiders, the introduction of cloth, cookware, guns, and other items began to transform the Native American way of life.

Hernando de Soto and other Spanish explorers passed through current-day Oklahoma searching for gold.

The Native People

The name "Oklahoma" comes from the Choctaw phrase "oklah homma," which means "red people." The Choctaw were not the first native people to live in this region, however. When the first European settlers arrived, they found several Native American tribes already living in there. These included the Plains Apache, Arapaho, Caddo, Comanche, Kiowa, Osage, Quapaw, and Wichita tribes.

The Caddo and Wichita people may be the oldest inhabitants of the state, as they were descendants of the Mound Builders. Like their forefathers, they lived in villages and raised corn, beans, pumpkins, and melons. The people of the Osage and Quapaw tribes were also much alike. Their forefathers were members of the same tribe and they spoke the same language, but with slight differences in dialect. Other tribes like the Comanche lived very differently, moving frequently to find better hunting grounds. Some of the Native American tribes lived at peace with one another, while others fought for land, food or power.

As more Europeans arrived in the US, other tribes **migrated** into Oklahoma, displacing most of the earlier peoples. These included the Osages, Pawnees, Kiowas, Comanches, Delawares, Shawnees, and Kickapoos. The Indian Removal Act of 1830 forced more Native Americans to relocate to the area, including the Choctaws, Cherokees, Creeks, Chickasaws and Seminoles—the "Five Civilized Tribes." When even more settlers entered the area after the Civil War, the federal government moved other Native Americans from Kansas and Nebraska reservations and relocated them in the Indian Territory.

Today there are more than 321,000 Native Americans living in Oklahoma, making

The Village of the Kiowa Tribe was painted in the nineteenth century by Baldwin Mollhausen.

up nearly 9 percent of the total population. Twenty-five different Native American languages are spoken, more than any other state. Oklahoma also has the largest diversity of Native American tribes in the United States with thirty-eight federally recognized tribes located within its borders. Federally recognized tribes have a government-to-government relationship with the United States and are eligible for funding and services from the Bureau of Indian Affairs. They also have certain rights of self-government (tribal sovereignty) and are entitled to receive certain federal benefits, services, and protections because of their special relationship with the United States.

Spotlight on the Kiowa

Kiowa is pronounced "kye-oh-wuh," a poor English pronunciation of their own tribal name, Gaigwu. The Kiowa Native Americans are the original people of Colorado, New Mexico, Oklahoma, and Texas. The Kiowa tribe was forced to move to a reservation in Oklahoma during the 1800s, and most Kiowa people are still living in Oklahoma today.

Homes: The Kiowa lived in large buffalo-hide tents called tipis (or teepees). Tipis were carefully designed to set up and break down quickly so an entire village could be ready to move within an hour.

Government: The Kiowa Nation has its own government, laws, police, and services, just like a small country. In the past, each Kiowa band was led by a chief. Today, the Kiowa tribe is governed by council members elected by the tribe. Kiowas are also US citizens and must obey American law.

Clothing: Kiowa women wore long deerskin dresses painted with yellow and green tribal designs. Kiowa men wore breechcloths and leather leggings, and usually went shirtless. The Kiowas wore moccasins on their feet. In cold weather, they wore long buffalo-hide robes.

Language: Most Kiowa people speak English today. Many Kiowas, especially elders, also speak their native Kiowa language but most children aren't learning it anymore. Some Kiowa people are working to keep their language alive.

Food: In addition to buffalo meat, the Kiowa ate small game like birds and rabbits, wild potatoes, fruits, and nuts.

Crafts: Kiowa artists are famous for their beadwork, hide paintings, and parfleche (decorated rawhide containers).

The Trail of Tears

In the 1830s and 1840s, the US government took actions against Native Americans in the eastern United States that would affect the Oklahoma region for decades to come. The government began a campaign to remove certain Native American groups from the southeastern states and relocate them to land west of the Mississippi River. The Cherokee, Choctaw, Chickasaw, Creek, and Seminole peoples—known as the Five Civilized Tribes— had made parts of Georgia, Florida, and Alabama their home for hundreds of years. Now they were forced to leave their homeland behind and enter the strange new landscape of the Great Plains. To prepare for the large number of newcomers, federal officials built Fort Towson, Fort Gibson, and other facilities in what is now Oklahoma.

Few of the Native Americans came of their own free will. In 1838–1839, thousands of Cherokee were moved to the unclaimed "no-man's-land" of the southern plains. Much of the journey was made in harsh winter weather, and there were shortages of food and other supplies. About four thousand Cherokee died while making this hard journey, now known as the Trail of Tears. The survivors eventually settled on the hills and plains of present-day Eastern Oklahoma. There, they set about the hard work of rebuilding their communities

Thousands of Cherokee died in the forced migration known as the Trail of Tears.

and their lives. Forced migrations of Native American groups continued into the 1840s.

All of what is now Oklahoma, except for the Panhandle (which in 1836 was claimed by the newly independent Texas Republic), was set aside by the US government for Native Americans. The area became known as Indian Territory or Indian Country. Over time, the relocated groups settled into their new homeland, where they organized their own new nations. They built homes and schools and established courts and legislatures, or groups that set up tribal laws. The Cherokee and Choctaw grew cotton, while the Creek and Chickasaw mostly herded livestock.

The Civil War and Beyond

From 1861 to 1865, states from the North and states from the South fought against each other in the Civil War. During this war, no major battles took place in Oklahoma, although several skirmishes occurred there.

Loyalties in the region were divided. Having been relocated from the South, some of the Native Americans had African-American slaves. The South supported slavery so, when it came time to choose sides, a majority of the Native Americans supported the South, which was also called the Confederacy. At first, the Cherokee were reluctant to favor either the Union (the North) or the Confederacy. But representatives from the Confederate states of Texas and Arkansas met with them, urging them to support the South. Eventually the Cherokee Nation agreed to side with the Confederacy.

The decision to support the South in the Civil War cost these Native Americans dearly. After being forced to move from their traditional lands to the new territory, the Native American tribes had started to adapt to their new surroundings. Their lives had improved due to a better economy and more cooperation among the tribes. The decision to side with the Confederacy led to more disagreements among the tribes, some of which wanted to support the North or not choose sides. It also angered the North, especially when Native American troops joined the South in fighting the Union.

When the Union won the Civil War, Oklahoma's Native American nations were punished by the government for having supported the losing side. The western part of

Making a Kiowa Tipi

Many Native American tribes made tipis (also spelled tepees or teepees) from long tree limbs and animal hides. You can make a wonderful model tipi using a brown paper grocery bag and twigs.

What You Need

Four straight twigs (about 1 foot long or 30.5 cm each)

Yarn, twine, or a rubber band

A large, brown paper grocery bag

Scissors

A pencil

Crayons, tempera paint, or markers

Tape

What to Do

- Bind the twigs together toward the top using yarn, string, or a rubber band. Leave about 3 inches (7.6 cm) of twig at one side of the string. Do not bind the twigs too tightly.
- Gently adjust the twigs so that they form a tipi shape.
- Holding the tipi above a piece of scrap paper, trace the outline of one side of the tipi. This will be your template for making the tipi. Cut out your triangular template.
- Open up a large paper bag along its seams. Lay your triangle template on the opened bag and trace its outline.
- Trace the triangle three more times with the long edges touching.
- Cut out this large polygon along the outside edge. Cut a door on one edge. Decorate the tipi using crayons or markers.
- Fold the paper along each of the pencil lines. Then form the paper into a tipi shape and tape the edges together.

- Snip off the top of the tipi (the twigs will go through this hole).
- Put the twigs into the tipi. Tape the twigs into place—each twig is taped along a fold line. You now have a wonderful tipi!

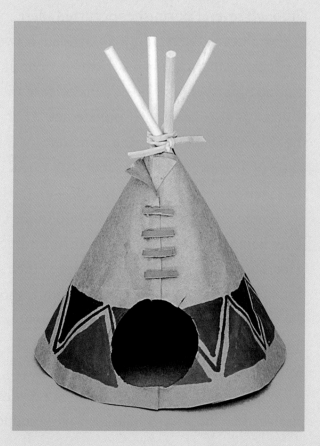

Cattle drives passed through what is now Oklahoma on the way to railroad lines.

Indian Territory, which had originally been granted to the Five Civilized Tribes, was taken away from them and divided among other Native American groups. The Peoria, Ottawa, Wyandot, and Miami tribes began farming on **reservations** established for them in the area. Cheyenne, Kiowa, Comanche, and Arapaho Native Americans, who were used to the wide-open spaces of the plains, had more difficulty adjusting to the often-cramped living conditions on the reservations.

In 1865, the United States signed the Little Arkansas Treaties with the Kiowa, Comanche, Cheyenne, and Arapaho tribes. The Native American nations agreed to remain peaceful and to limit the size of their hunting ranges. In exchange, the US government vowed to protect and support the tribes. The treaties promised the Native Americans the power to own and govern their new homelands. But the US government was not concerned with honoring these rights. Two years later, the Treaty of Medicine Lodge Creek greatly reduced Native American rights to their lands.

After the Civil War, the flow of white settlers onto the southern plains also increased. Soon the newcomers pushed up against the borders of the Indian territories. Non-Native American people, seeking a new and better life along the American frontier, flooded into the area. The unclaimed expanses of free land surrounding Native American Territory were soon taken. To make matters worse, hunters—mostly from the eastern United States—killed tens of thousands of bison, taking away an important food source from the Native Americans in the region.

Red All Over

Red dirt is found on more than 1 million acres [404,685 ha] in thirty-three counties in Oklahoma. The dirt is red because of the weathering of sands, siltstone, and shale.

Tent cities, along with offices for
attorneys, sprang up when former Indian
lands were opened for settlement.

The Changing Plains

With the arrival of so many new people, the region's economy began to expand. The area
became a crossroads for the many cattle herds being moved from the ranches of Texas
to railroad lines in Kansas. Ranchers drove their herds across what is now Oklahoma,
pausing to fatten the valuable animals on the grasses of the plains. While some cattlemen
paid the Native Americans for the right to have their herds graze on Native American–
held lands, most did not.

Soon, several well-traveled cattle trails crossed the region. The Chisholm Trail became
the best known, but the Western, East Shawnee, and West Shawnee trails were also heavily
used. Between 1866 and 1885, more than six million head of Texas longhorn cattle crossed
Native American lands. Slowly, ranchers became convinced of the value of owning what
was once considered bleak and useless land.

When the railroad came to Oklahoma in the early 1870s, the region became even
more valuable in the eyes of ranchers and other settlers. At first it was difficult for the
railroad companies to put tracks in Oklahoma, since they did not have rights to build on
Native American land. A treaty signed in 1866 allowed one north-south and one east-west
railroad to be built through territories. By the 1880s, the rules concerning Indian Territory
were seen more and more as a barrier to trade and Congress began to allow further
railroad construction through Oklahoma.

Land of Man-Made Lakes

Oklahoma has more man-made lakes [two hundred] than any other state, more than one million surface-acres of water, and two thousand more miles of shoreline than the Atlantic and Gulf coasts combined.

Boomers and Sooners

By the late 1800s, many settlers were eager to claim Native American lands for themselves. Called Boomers, these settlers were led by William L. Couch, Charles C. Carpenter, and David L. Payne. They put pressure on the US government to open the Indian Territory lands for settlement by others.

Eventually, the government yielded. From the Creek and the Seminole, it bought more than 3 million acres (1.2 million ha). This parcel was added to lands taken from other Native American nations. A large part of what is now Central Oklahoma was then declared open for settlement in 1889. On April 22, eager land-grabbers lined up along the border, awaiting the signal to head into the so-called Unassigned Lands. At noon, the Unassigned Lands were officially opened. The signal brought a mad dash as settlers raced into the unclaimed area. They were in search of a prime stretch of countryside to call their own. Those who had sneaked into the territory illegally, before the official signal, were known as Sooners. Oklahoma residents have been nicknamed Sooners ever since.

Indian Territory and Oklahoma Territory

The Oklahoma region had been known since the 1830s as Indian Territory or Indian Country. This changed on May 2, 1890, when the region was divided into two parts. One was still called Indian Territory, while the other was named the Oklahoma Territory. Indian Territory included the remaining lands of the Five Civilized Tribes plus the limited holdings of other tribes. The Oklahoma Territory included the former Unassigned Lands, along with the Panhandle (then known as No Man's Land), which had earlier belonged to Texas. George Washington Steele was named the Oklahoma Territory's first governor.

The largest land rush in the history of the Oklahoma Territory took place on September 16, 1893. That was the day a huge tract of land in the north-central part of the region was first opened to non-Native American settlers. Most of this land consisted of what was known as the Cherokee Outlet, an area the Native Americans had essentially been forced to sell to the US government at a very low price. When this land became available to settlers, more than fifty thousand people descended on the region.

Oklahoma City

Lawton

1. Oklahoma City: population 579,999

Ten thousand homesteaders settled Oklahoma City during a historic land run on April 22, 1889. Located at the convergence of three major highways, Oklahoma City is a principal distribution center within the state and the southwest region.

2. Tulsa: population 391,906

Tulsa is nestled in the northeastern quadrant of Oklahoma, surrounded by rolling green hills and wooded terrain. The city boasts a widely diversified business base and the Tulsa Port of Catoosa is one of the country's largest river ports.

3. Norman: population 110,925

Norman was primarily developed as a headquarters for the Santa Fe Railroad, which helped the city to flourish. In 1890, Norman was chosen as the location for the University of Oklahoma (OU). The Norman campus has an enrollment of approximately twenty-two thousand.

4. Broken Arrow: population 98,850

Broken Arrow, a suburb of Tulsa, was settled by the Creek tribe, which named it after its original home in Alabama. Before the city became a suburb, its economy was based on agriculture.

5. Lawton: population 96,867

Lawton is located 90 miles (145 km) southwest of Oklahoma City. The Fort Sill Army Post and the Wichita Mountains National Wildlife Refuge are both located nearby. Lawton is on Forbes Magazine's list of the Best Small Places for Business and Careers.

OKLAHOMA ★ ★ ★

6. Edmond: population 81,405

Just north of Oklahoma City, Edmond is located on scenic Route 66 and is close to attractions such as the National Cowboy and Western Heritage Museum, Remington Park horse racing, and historic and picturesque Guthrie.

7. Moore: population 55,081

Moore's close proximity to the state's capital city on the north and the University of Oklahoma to the south make the city an attractive, convenient place to live, although it has also been the site of several devastating tornadoes.

8. Midwest City: population 54,371

A prominent Oklahoma businessman founded Midwest City in 1942 after he learned of the Army's desire to build a military base in the area. The city's economy still revolves around what is now called Tinker Air Force Base.

9. Enid: population 49,379

Enid lies at the intersection of the Chisholm Trail and Cherokee Strip Land Run. Oil and agriculture have always been major components of the city's economy and Enid still boasts the world's third largest grain storage capacity. Vance Air Force Base is located nearby.

10. Stillwater: population 45,688

Stillwater was founded soon after the Oklahoma Territory's Unassigned Lands opened for settlement. Its economy is diverse and includes its largest employer, Oklahoma State University. *Money* magazine chose Stillwater as one of its 100 top places to live in 2010.

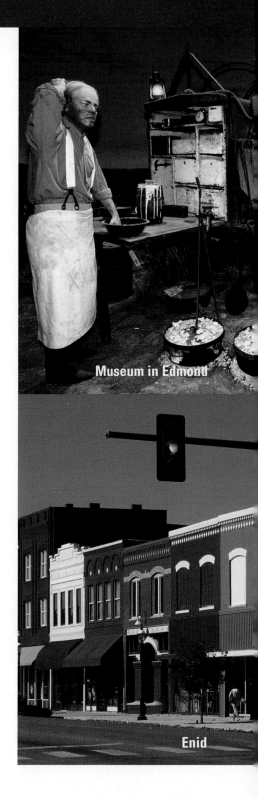

Museum in Edmond

Enid

Many of the newcomers, who were known as homesteaders, were not prepared for the hard life they faced on the open plains. All they saw was free land and not the challenges and responsibilities that came with it. For every farm or ranch that succeeded, many others failed. Many homesteaders abandoned their plots of land.

Wealthy landowners, often called land barons, then bought up these abandoned homesteads. By the late 1890s, many settlers who arrived in the region found there was only land to rent, not own. By 1900, 40 percent of Oklahoma's farmers were tenant farmers. These tenant farmers rented the land from the owner and paid the landowner a portion of their crops in exchange. This arrangement between tenant farmers and landowners was known as **sharecropping**.

Cimarron's Special

Cimarron County is the only county in the United States that touches four states: Colorado, New Mexico, Texas, and Kansas.

The Path to Statehood

In 1893, a group called the Dawes Commission was set up to divide some of the remaining Native American lands into smaller pieces. These parcels of land in Indian Territory were to go to Native American families or individuals rather than tribes. US officials saw the program as a way of reducing what little control some Native American nations still had over their tracts of land. Agents helped the Native Americans set up towns and prepare to become American citizens.

Slowly, Indian Territory became a mixture of white settlers and Native Americans who owned their own private plots of land. The population grew. By 1905, many people in Indian Territory believed it was ready for statehood. The Five Civilized Tribes called a constitutional **convention** at Muskogee. White settlers were invited to take part as well. They outnumbered the Native Americans by five to one. At the end of the convention, they all agreed to create the state of Sequoyah. The action was then approved by a majority of voters in Indian Territory.

The US Congress refused to consider the Sequoyah plan, however. Instead, federal officials wanted to create one state called Oklahoma out of both Indian Territory and the Oklahoma Territory. Delegates from both territories met in Guthrie in 1906.

The discovery of oil in the early 1900s helped Oklahoma's economy boom.

They agreed to combine the two territories, and on November 16, 1907, Oklahoma officially became a state. At the time, its population totaled more than 1.4 million. Guthrie was named the first state capital. Three years later, the capital was moved to Oklahoma City.

In the first decade of the 1900s, the state's economy boomed, largely because of a growing oil industry. After early oil finds at Chelsea in 1889 and Bartlesville in 1897, the opening of the Red Fork oil field in 1901 made Tulsa the center of Oklahoma's oil business. Cattle ranching, though on the decline, remained a major source of the state's income. At the same time, crops such as corn, wheat, and cotton added to Oklahoma's wealth. But farming was still a hard life for many of Oklahoma's residents.

War and Racial Violence

In 1917, the United States entered World War I (1914–1918). About ninety-one thousand Oklahomans served in the military during the conflict. More than one thousand troops from Oklahoma were killed in action, and about 4,500 were wounded.

During wartime, demand increased for crops and food products, which Oklahoma's farmers helped to supply. But after this short period of prosperity, the state's fortunes took a turn for the worse. Farm prices dropped, making it hard for farmers to earn a living. The Ku Klux Klan (KKK), an organization that supported violence against African Americans and other minorities, gained popularity across the state. The Klan's influence spread to city and county governments, in which some KKK members held important positions.

In 1921, in one of Tulsa's darkest moments, angry white mobs threatened to kill an African-American man falsely accused of hurting a white woman. When residents of

African Americans arrested in the racial violence in Tulsa in 1921 are dropped off to receive treatment for their wounds.

Woody Guthrie gave a voice to the people of the Dust Bowl.

the African-American neighborhood of Greenwood resisted, a gun battle erupted, and many buildings were set ablaze. As many as three hundred African Americans were killed, and most of the Greenwood neighborhood was destroyed.

Dust Bowl Days

When farm prices fell after World War I, farmers tried to plant more crops to make up for their losses, but this only made matters worse. The overworked soil yielded poorer harvests. At the same time, overgrazing by the state's many cattle removed much of the grass from Oklahoma's rangelands. This further weakened the quality of Oklahoma's soil.

By the beginning of the 1930s, the nation was in the grips of the Great Depression. During this period of economic hardship, millions of Americans could not find jobs and families struggled to survive. Banks closed, taking people's life savings with them.

In Oklahoma, extremely hot summers and lack of rainfall made matters worse. Crops withered and died in the fields. Drought spread across the plains. High winds raised huge clouds of dust. At times, the clouds were so large and thick they seemed to blot out the daylight. The American prairie became known as the Dust Bowl. Oklahoma was at the heart of it.

Giving voice to these people was folk singer Woody Guthrie. The Okemah native went on to become one of the most important folk singers in the history of the United States. His song "This Land is Your

A storm in Cimarron County in 1936 blows the soil from a farm.

The Fort Gibson Dam, which was completed in 1950, produced electricity and opportunities for recreation.

Land" has been called by some an alternative national anthem. He was inducted into the Oklahoma Hall of Fame in 2006.

Many of the state's farmers, ranchers, and other workers decided to leave. Okies, as they were called, moved west in the hope of leaving the hard times behind them. As a result, the state lost more than three hundred thousand residents. But times were hard everywhere else in the country as well.

Eventually the drought ended. People learned a harsh lesson from the Dust Bowl years and began to use the land more wisely. Aid from the federal government helped the state's economy recover. Between 1941 and 1945, while the United States was directly involved in World War II, demand grew for the state's two main products, crops and oil. Military bases, built outside of Enid and Oklahoma City, also created much-needed jobs.

Oklahoma after World War II

The second half of the twentieth century brought further changes. Dams and irrigation projects improved farmlands, provided electric power, and created lakes for recreation. Strong governors led the way in improving education, reforming prisons, and strengthening the ways the state handled its finances.

New industries and construction projects boosted the state's economy in the 1960s. Electronics plants were built in Oklahoma City. The state capital also became the home of a major center for the Federal Aviation Administration (FAA). This important FAA facility trained airport workers and conducted research into airplane safety. Farther east, Tulsa became the site of factories making parts for airplanes and spacecraft. Today, more than fourteen thousand people in the Tulsa area have jobs in the aerospace industry.

In the 1970s, Oklahoma's abundance of open land, fuel, water, and electric power continued to attract companies to the state. In 1971, the Oklahoma portion of the Arkansas River Navigation System opened. This made it easier for products from Muskogee and Tulsa to reach major US cities and ports.

During this decade, a dramatic rise in oil prices brought another boost to the state's income. But when oil prices declined in the 1980s, Oklahoma's economy experienced a steep drop. Oil wells across the state were shut down. During the 1990s, state leaders looked for ways to broaden the state's sources of income. New businesses were lured to Oklahoma, requiring workers trained in an ever-wider variety of skills. Tourism, technology, and educational and health services took on increased importance.

In recent years, the state has benefited from large increases in prices for oil and **natural gas** and the nation's desire to produce more energy at home. Oklahoma has become one of the nation's leading natural gas producers. When the nation's economy slowed late

Aerospace industries employ thousands of Oklahomans.

Rescue workers cut through the wreckage of the Oklahoma City bombing in 1995.

in 2007, Oklahoma fared better than many other states. Reversing a pattern set decades earlier, Oklahoma even began attracting people and jobs from California and other western states.

The Oklahoma City Bombing

On April 19, 1995, another dark chapter was added to the state's history. On a quiet morning in Oklahoma City, a truck filled with explosives blew up in front of the Alfred P. Murrah Federal Building. It was parked there by a man named Timothy McVeigh. The bombing killed 168 Oklahomans, including 19 young children in a child-care center on the building's first floor. More than 500 other people were injured.

McVeigh escaped but was later arrested. He was convicted in 1997 of murder and other crimes, and he was put to death four years later. An accomplice, Terry Nichols, is serving life in prison. A memorial built at the site where the building once stood has attracted millions of visitors since it opened in 2000. It ensures that people will never forget those who lost their lives because of this **terrorist** act.

10 KEY DATES IN STATE HISTORY

1. 12,000–10,000 BCE

People of the Clovis culture hunt mammoths and other large mammals. Their artifacts can still be found throughout Oklahoma.

2. April 1541

Spanish explorer Francisco Vásquez de Coronado leaves the area of New Mexico in search of gold and becomes the first European to enter present-day Oklahoma.

3. April 30, 1803

In the Louisiana Purchase, the United States buys a huge area of land from France that includes what is now Oklahoma.

4. June 30, 1834

US Congress passes the Indian Intercourse Act. It establishes an area known as Indian Territory to which the Five Civilized Tribes are relocated.

5. April 22, 1889

The Oklahoma land rush begins as the US government opens up the Unassigned Lands of Indian Territory to settlement. Thousands of homesteaders stake claims.

6. November 16, 1907

Oklahoma becomes the forty-sixth state. The new state combines both the Oklahoma and the Indian territories, which had been established in 1890.

7. May 31, 1921

Racial violence in the Greenwood District of Tulsa claims up to three hundred African-American lives and destroys more than one thousand homes and businesses.

8. April 14, 1935

A major sandstorm, dubbed "The Black Blizzard," ravages Oklahoma during the Dust Bowl era, when severe drought and high winds dried out the soil.

9. April 19, 1995

Two American terrorists detonate a truck bomb and destroy the Alfred P. Murrah Federal Building in Oklahoma City, killing 168 people, including nineteen children.

10. November 5, 2011

The strongest **earthquake** in Oklahoma's history, measuring 5.6 on the Richter scale, occurs near Oklahoma City. Luckily there are no serious injuries.

Members of many tribes wear traditional
clothing at the Pow-Wow of Champions in Tulsa.

The People

When Oklahoma became the forty-sixth state in 1907, its residents were already a blend of many cultures and traditions. Oklahomans included cotton farmers from the South, wheat farmers from the Midwest, and cattle ranchers from the West. Native Americans, African Americans, and people of European descent were all part of the population. While many people had come to farm the land, by the twentieth century others were drawn by the rise of the petroleum industry.

Native Americans

Nearly 10 percent of all Native Americans now living in the United States make their homes in Oklahoma. The state government recognizes nearly forty Native American nations located within the state. Most Oklahoma Native Americans live in and around Tulsa and Oklahoma City, but many still live on reservations and in small communities throughout the state.

Oklahoma's Native Americans have made many efforts to develop local businesses and to keep Native American culture and traditions alive. In recent years, the leaders of Native American nations have encouraged their members to take a more active role in Oklahoma politics and government. The first steps are registering to vote and being counted in the census. These actions are designed to impress on state officials the voting strength and economic power of the state's Native American communities.

A Mix of European Cultures

When coal mines were opened near McAlester in the late 1800s, European immigrants flooded into the region. Newcomers from Wales, Ireland, Poland, Russia, Italy, France, and Lithuania made the McAlester area one of the most diverse in the territory.

Other groups created their own towns on the plains. German Mennonites brought sacks of Crimean hard wheat to their new American homes. They started farming communities named Corn, Colony, and Bessie in Western Oklahoma. Czech immigrants, mostly arriving from other parts of the Midwest, settled in towns such as Prague, Yukon, and Mishak.

In recent years, new groups have arrived. They are adding to the changing face of Oklahoma. No matter how diverse the newcomers may be, most of them are drawn to the state for similar reasons. Community pride, good schools, and a slower pace of life help make the Sooner State a great place to live.

Hispanic Americans and Asian Americans

Oklahoma's Hispanic population more than tripled between 1990 and 2010, and Hispanic Americans now make up about 9 percent of the state's population. Most Hispanics in Oklahoma are of Mexican origin. Others are of Puerto Rican or Cuban heritage. The

Hispanics, a growing minority, march for greater rights in Oklahoma City.

growth of the Hispanic population has been concentrated in and around the state's major cities. Hispanics make up about 17 percent of the population in Oklahoma City and 14 percent in Tulsa.

Oklahoma City, with about 580,000 people, is the largest city in the state, and Tulsa, with about 390,000 people, is the second largest. Hispanic Americans in Oklahoma work in many careers and run many types of businesses. In Tulsa's Little Mexico neighborhood, restaurants and food stores offer people of all cultures a taste of Mexican cooking and traditional foods.

Although they still account for less than 2 percent of the state's total population, Asian Americans represent one of Oklahoma's fastest-growing minority groups. Growth in the hog farming and processing industries has helped to attract some of the newcomers, who include thousands of people of Vietnamese heritage. After the Vietnam War ended in the mid-1970s, a large number of Vietnamese families came to the United States. But moving to the United States from Vietnam was expensive, and often relatives had to be left behind. Beginning in the late 1970s, Oklahoma welcomed a new wave of Vietnamese immigrants, reuniting families that had been divided during the first wave of immigration.

Oklahoma was a haven for African Americans seeking opportunities.

African Americans

The 2010 Census counted more than 277,000 African Americans in Oklahoma. Most of the first black Oklahomans were slaves owned by members of the Five Civilized Tribes. When the Native Americans were forced west along the Trail of Tears, their slaves came with them.

During the Civil War, escaped slaves and people of mixed race, usually of both black and Native American heritage, played key roles in the Union's success. One historically important event was the Battle of Honey Springs, fought on July 17, 1863, outside present-day Muskogee. The battle, which was won by the Union, marked the first time regiments of whites, blacks, and Native Americans fought on the same field. The First Kansas Colored Volunteer Infantry Regiment, as well as Native American regiments, joined white Union troops to win the day.

After the Civil War, Congress created the all-black Ninth and Tenth Cavalries. Made up mostly of veterans of the war, they were stationed in the Oklahoma region at Forts Gibson and Sill. These troops, known as buffalo soldiers, performed many roles on the frontier. They helped build new forts, fought the many bandits hiding out in the territory, and helped move Sooners off land they had illegally seized.

★ 10 KEY PEOPLE ★

Ralph Ellison

Mickey Mantle

Brad Pitt

1. Ralph Ellison

Oklahoma City's Ralph Ellison became the first African American to win the National Book Award. His novel *Invisible Man* tells the story of an African-American man losing his identity in a racist world. Some think it is one of the best American novels of the twentieth century

2. Ron Howard

The Duncan native was a child star on the *Andy Griffith Show* and later on Happy Days. He moved on to directing, making movies such as *Splash, Parenthood, Willow,* and *Apollo 13* before winning two Academy Awards and a Golden Globe for *A Beautiful Mind.*

3. Shannon Lucid

Shannon Lucid was born in China but grew up in Bethany. She was one of the first six women chosen by NASA to be an astronaut and flew on five missions, for a total of 223 days in space.

4. Mickey Mantle

Born in Spavinaw in 1931, this switch-hitting center fielder starred for eighteen years with the New York Yankees. Mickey Mantle won three Most Valuable Player awards and was elected to the Baseball Hall of Fame.

5. Brad Pitt

Born in Shawnee, Brad Pitt has acted in many films, including *Legends of the Fall, Moneyball*, and *World War Z.* He won a Best Picture Oscar in 2014 as a producer for *12 Years a Slave.*

OKLAHOMA ★ ★ ★

6. Will Rogers

Part Cherokee, Will Rogers was born on a ranch in Oologah, Indian Territory, in 1879. He dropped out of high school to be a cowboy but eventually became one of the nation's most popular movie stars, authors, and political humorists.

7. Maria Tallchief

Born in 1925 in Fairfax to Scottish-Irish and Native American parents, Maria Tallchief studied music and dance in California. She married choreographer George Balanchine and became prima ballerina of the New York City Ballet.

8. Jim Thorpe

Legendary Native American Jim Thorpe was born near Prague. A football All-American at the Carlisle Indian School, he won the pentathlon and decathlon at the 1912 Olympics before his gold medals were revoked on a technicality. Thorpe also played professional baseball and football.

9. Carrie Underwood

Carrie Underwood was born in Muskogee and grew up in Checotah. In 2005 she earned top honors on television's *American Idol*. She then won a Grammy Award as Best New Artist in 2007 and remains one of country music's biggest stars.

10. Alfre Woodard

Born in Tulsa, Alfre Woodard was a high school cheerleader and track star. She began acting after being persuaded to audition by a nun at her school. Woodard is the most honored African-American actress in Primetime Emmy Award history.

Will Rogers

Maria Tallchief

Carrie Underwood

Who Oklahomans Are

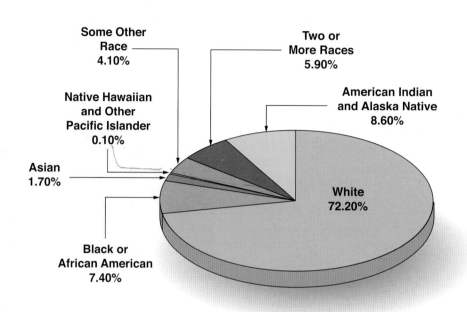

Some Other Race 4.10%

Two or More Races 5.90%

Native Hawaiian and Other Pacific Islander 0.10%

American Indian and Alaska Native 8.60%

Asian 1.70%

White 72.20%

Black or African American 7.40%

Total Population 3,751,351

Hispanic or Latino (of any race):
- 332,007 people (8.90%)

Note: The pie chart shows the racial breakdown of the state's population based on the categories used by the U.S. Bureau of the Census. The Census Bureau reports information for Hispanics or Latinos separately, since they may be of any race. Percentages in the pie chart may not add to 100 because of rounding.

Source: US Bureau of the Census, 2010 Census

Later, African Americans came to the region as farmers, cowboys, and businesspeople. From 1865 to 1920, African Americans in Oklahoma created more than fifty all-black towns, some of which still exist. For people escaping the shadow of slavery, Oklahoma was seen as a kind of paradise. African Americans could vote, study, and work with greater ease and freedom than in most other states. Black Oklahomans were also encouraged to start businesses, which they did in great numbers.

In Tulsa, the mostly African-American section of town called Greenwood was also known as the Black Wall Street. Developed by a rich landowner named O. W. Gurley, Greenwood's thirty-five blocks were home to more than eleven thousand residents. Some of them were prosperous business owners and millionaires.

Unfortunately, Greenwood is now remembered as the location of what many believe to be the single worst incident of racial violence in American history. On May 31, 1921, the arrest of a young black man on a questionable charge of assaulting a young white woman touched off a deadly riot. For eighteen hours, whites charged through the community in retaliation, leaving an estimated three hundred people dead, another ten thousand black residents homeless, and thirty-five city blocks in ruin. The bloody race riot has continued to haunt Oklahomans to the present day.

After the riot, black Oklahomans rebuilt Greenwood, and by the early 1940s, the district was once again home to more than 240 businesses that were owned or operated by African Americans. Today, Oklahoma's black community is as strong as ever.

Arts and Culture

Oklahoma culture has been influenced by the wide variety of backgrounds of its people. Europeans with English, Scottish, Irish, German, and Czech heritage have mixed with Native Americans, African Americans, Hispanics, and others. So many Native Americans were forced to move to Oklahoma when settlers moved into their traditional lands that Oklahoma now leads all states in language diversity.

Traditional dance is among the cultural arts kept alive at the Czech Festival in Yukon.

Western ranchers, Native American tribes, southern settlers, and eastern oil barons have shaped the state's arts and culture to the point that its largest cities have been named among the most underrated cultural destinations in the United States. Oklahoma City's Festival of the Arts has been named one of the top fine arts festivals in the nation. The state has produced musical styles such as The Tulsa Sound and Western Swing. Oklahoma City offers prominent theatre companies such as Carpenter Square Theatre and Oklahoma Shakespeare in the Park. In Tulsa, Oklahoma's oldest resident professional company is the American Theatre Company, and Theatre Tulsa is the oldest community theatre company west of the Mississippi. The cities of Norman, Lawton, and Stillwater also host well-reviewed community theatre companies.

Oklahoma contains more than three hundred museums. The Sam Noble Oklahoma Museum of Natural History in Norman is one of the largest university-based art and history museums in the country. The Gilcrease Museum in Tulsa holds one of the world's largest collections of art and artifacts of the American West.

Annual ethnic festivals and events take place throughout the state. These include Native American powwows and festivals celebrating Scottish, Irish, German, Italian, Vietnamese, Chinese, Czech, Jewish, Arab, Mexican, and African-American culture and traditions.

Each year, the State Fair of Oklahoma (held in Oklahoma City) and the Tulsa State Fair attract around one million people each. Norman hosts the Norman Music Festival, which highlights native Oklahoma bands and musicians.

Education

More than 186,000 students are enrolled in public higher education in Oklahoma. More than thirty thousand students are enrolled at the University of Oklahoma in Norman. Other large colleges and universities include Tulsa Community College (about twenty thousand students) and Oklahoma State University in Stillwater (nearly twenty-six thousand students). The US Chamber of Commerce Foundation ranks Oklahoma's system of higher education as the fifth most affordable in the nation.

Higher education in Oklahoma is also big business. Expenditures of the Oklahoma public higher education system generate $9.2 billion in economic benefit in the state and support more than eighty-five thousand Oklahoma jobs.

Sports

Oklahoma hosts one major league professional sports team. The Oklahoma City Thunder is a top-ranked team in the National Basketball Association (NBA) and features star players including Kevin Durant and Russell Westbrook. The other professional sports team is the Oklahoma City Dodgers, the Triple-A affiliate for the Los Angeles Dodgers of major league baseball (MLB). The Tulsa Oilers are members of the East Coast Hockey League. College sports are very big in Oklahoma. The University of Oklahoma Sooners average more than eighty-five thousand fans for each football game, and the Oklahoma State Cowboys average close to sixty thousand. The Sooners have won nine national championships since the start of the twenty-first century, five in men's gymnastics and one in women's gymnastics. The Cowboys have won five over the same period. The National Wrestling Hall of Fame is located in Stillwater.

Many Forms of Faith

Oklahoma's religious profile is very different than those in other parts of the nation. Such differences stem from the state's unique history and remain a major shaper of its people and institutions. Oklahomans identify themselves as Southern Baptist almost seven times more often than other Americans, while Churches of Christ, Methodist, Pentecostal, and Holiness groups are also much more common in Oklahoma than elsewhere.

Correspondingly, Oklahomans are much less often associated with mainstream Protestant churches, Roman Catholicism, and Judaism. The mix of faiths is made even richer by the continuing strength of Native American spirituality and religious influences.

Tornado Alley and Dixie Alley

One thing all Oklahomans have to deal with is sudden changes in the weather. In addition to violent thunderstorms and dry conditions, another weather-related disaster that can break the relative summer calm is a tornado.

During the summer, the plains of Middle America get very hot (creating updrafts) and there are many thunderstorms. Tornadoes form during thunderstorms, when unstable hot air near the ground rises and meets the cooler air above in the thunder clouds.

Tornadoes are a possibility in Oklahoma from late spring though the fall.

Climate scientists classify Oklahoma as part of two separate tornado regions. The first region is Tornado Alley, which extends from Texas northward to South Dakota. This area gets most of its tornadoes in late spring. The second region is Dixie Alley, which ranges from eastern Texas and Oklahoma across the Deep South. In this area, tornadoes typically occur in late fall.

Oklahoma averages about fifty tornadoes each year, but the number can swing widely from one year to the next. In 1999, Oklahoma experienced 144 tornadoes, while in 1988 there were only 17. Tornadoes can be deadly and can cause huge amounts of property damage. The most deadly tornado to ever strike Oklahoma occurred on Wednesday, April 9, 1947 near Woodward, killing at least 116 people in the state. The massive May 20, 2013 tornado that pulverized the city of Moore had peak winds estimated at 210 miles per hour (340 kilometers per hour). It killed 24 people and injured more than 370 others.

89er Days Celebration

Mangum Rattlesnake Derby

1. American Heritage Music Festival

Cloggers (folk dancers) and fiddlers come to Grove each June to compete for cash prizes and the right to claim the title of grand champion. This weekend full of dancing and music is capped off by special performances each evening.

2. Arbuckle Mountain Bluegrass Festival

Head to Wynnewood in September for food, fun, and bluegrass music. Festivalgoers are treated to some of the best bluegrass musicians performing today, plus some talented newcomers.

3. Chuck Wagon Gathering and Children's Cowboy Festival

Each May in Oklahoma City, you can experience cowboy and frontier life. Learn how to make rope, ride in a real wagon, and try a Shetland pony carousel. There are also authentic foods prepared by **chuck wagon** crews.

4. Czech Festival

This event celebrating Czech culture and traditions is held in Yukon on the first weekend in October. The festival includes a parade up Main Street, carnival rides, music and dancing, craft displays, and traditional Czech foods.

5. 89er Days Celebration

The Oklahoma Territory Land Run of April 22, 1889, has been commemorated in Guthrie, Oklahoma for more than one hundred years. The Celebration includes a parade, carnival, chuck wagon feast, rodeo, and an old-timers' baseball game. Both a queen and a princess are crowned.

6. Mangum Rattlesnake Derby

Each April, participants in the annual Mangum Rattlesnake Derby compete to find the longest snake. Visitors who prefer tamer pastimes can enjoy a live snake show, snack on fried rattlesnake, or have a photo taken with a genuine live rattler.

7. Oklahoma State Fair

The fair has been a hugely popular event for over a century and is recognized as "Oklahoma's Premier Family Attraction." Events include performances by famous musicians, live rodeo competitions, livestock showing, and bull riding.

8. Poteau Balloon Fest

Hot-air balloons hover over the town of Poteau every October. But this festival is more than just balloons. With mud pit races, stagecoach rides, a pet costume contest, skydivers, helicopter rides, and Native American dancers, this event offers something for everyone.

9. Red Earth Native American Cultural Festival

Each June, Oklahoma City plays host to the largest Native American event of its kind. The festival features works by more than 1,200 Native American artists and dancers, and a grand parade representing more than one hundred Native American nations.

10. Woody Guthrie Folk Festival

This annual event, also known as WoodyFest, kicks off each July in Okemah, Woody Guthrie's hometown. It was started to honor his legacy. Folk, alternative, and acoustic performers provide the entertainment.

Poteau Balloon Fest

Red Earth Native American Cultural Festival

A tribute to Native Americans was dedicated in front of the state capitol building in 1989.

How the Government Works

Oklahoma's constitution was adopted in 1907, when Oklahoma became a state. The constitution and other state laws provide for multiple levels of government.

Oklahoma's state government consists of the legislative branch, which passes laws; the executive branch, which carries out the laws; and the judicial branch, which interprets the laws and administers justice. The state has seventy-seven counties. Every county has a county "seat," usually a large, centrally located town or village in the county, where the county government is based. State law also provides for the establishment of cities and towns, which have their own local government. Oklahoma's Native American nations choose their own leaders, who work together with state and federal government officials.

Branches of Government

Executive

The governor heads the state's executive branch. He or she is chosen by the state's voters to serve a four-year term and may serve no more than two terms in a row. Voters also choose key officials who help the governor run the state. They include the lieutenant governor, attorney general, and secretary of state.

Legislators gather in this room in the capitol to vote on bills.

Legislative

Oklahoma's state legislature is made up of two parts, or houses. The State Senate has forty-eight members, each elected to a four-year term. The State House Of Representatives is larger, with 101 members serving for two years each. Each lawmaker may not serve more than a combined total of twelve years in both houses of the legislature.

Judicial

The highest court in the state, the Supreme Court, has a chief justice and eight other justices. They are appointed by the governor and then approved by the state's voters to their six-year terms. The state also has a court of civil appeals, made up of at least twelve judges, and a court of criminal appeals, with five judges. Lower courts include district courts and municipal courts.

United States Senate and Congress

Like all other states, Oklahoma voters cast their ballots for president and vice president of the United States. They also choose people to represent them in the US Congress in Washington, DC. Oklahoma voters elect two US Senators and five representatives in the US House of Representatives.

Oklahoma Voters

More than two million people are registered to vote in Oklahoma. As of fall 2014, Democrats narrowly made up the largest percentage of Oklahoma voters at 43.8 percent. Republicans, at 43.6 percent, and Independents, at 12.6 percent, have seen growth in their ranks over the last few years.

Registrations for the two major political parties are closer than at any time since the state Election Board began compiling statewide voter registration data in 1960, when Democrats outnumbered Republicans 82 percent to 18 percent. In 1980, registrations were 76 percent Democratic and 23 percent Republican. In 2000, they were 57 percent Democratic and 35 percent Republican.

Despite the small lead in voter registration, Democratic candidates have struggled at the polls in recent years. In 2014, the governor was Republican, both chambers of the Oklahoma Legislature were controlled by Republicans, and Oklahoma's congressional delegation was all Republican.

Nations within a Nation

Like many other states, Oklahoma has tribal governments that are viewed as separate nations. Tribal governments have their own constitutions and can collect taxes, as well as pass laws and issue regulations concerning matters ranging from education to hunting rules to religion.

The Cherokee and other tribes have their own governments.

How a Bill Becomes a Law

Most Oklahoma laws start out as bills introduced by a state senator or representative. A bill is a proposed law. The legislator first presents the idea in written form. In most cases, the bill is then sent to a committee in the chamber where it is first introduced. The committee discusses the bill and may make changes to it.

Lawmakers serve on a variety of committees. Each committee focuses on a specific topic, such as transportation, finance, or the environment. People can attend some committee meetings and offer their views on the bill.

If the committee approves the bill, it is sent back to the chamber where it was introduced. The members of that chamber then have the chance to discuss the bill and make further changes. Finally, the bill comes up for a vote. If it passes, the bill goes to the other chamber of the legislature. There, the bill goes through a similar process. It is examined, debated, changed, and brought up for a vote. If the bill fails to pass in the second chamber, it cannot become law.

Often, the version of a bill that passes in the second chamber differs in important ways from the version that passed in the first one. In such cases, the bill is sent to a conference committee in which members of both chambers take part. The committee discusses the measure and works out a compromise version. This version is then submitted to the two separate chambers. If both chambers pass this final bill without further changes, it is sent to the governor. If the governor signs the bill, it then becomes law.

Sometimes, the legislature passes a bill that the governor opposes. In that case, the governor may reject, or veto, the measure. The bill then has one last chance to become law. It is returned to the legislature. If two-thirds of the members of each chamber vote to override the veto, the bill then passes despite the governor's opposition. After final passage, the measure is recorded, printed, and becomes an official part of Oklahoma law.

Initiative and Referendum

Most bills become law by gaining the approval of the legislature and the signature of the governor. But the state constitution offers Oklahomans two other, more direct methods to pass or change state laws. These methods are called initiative and referendum.

The initiative method allows people to propose new laws and constitutional changes, or amendments. Voters may then approve or reject the proposals at the next election. In order to qualify for the ballot, an initiative must receive a certain number of signatures on a petition, based on a specific percentage of the number of people who voted for governor at the previous election. To win approval, the proposal must be supported by a majority of people voting on that issue on Election Day.

Voters may approve laws or amendments on Election Day.

The other method that allows voters to have a direct say in approving or rejecting laws is called a referendum. When the legislature calls for a referendum, it gives voters a chance to accept or reject a new law before it takes effect. Voters may also propose a referendum to reject a law that has already been passed. As with voter initiatives, a certain number of signatures must be collected before a citizen-proposed referendum can get on the ballot. In order to pass, a referendum must gain a majority of those voting on that issue.

County and Local Government

County government in Oklahoma relies on commissioners. Each county is divided into districts, and each district elects a county commissioner. The commissioners work together to make sure county residents have access to services and programs. County residents also elect a sheriff to maintain law and order.

There are almost six hundred cities and towns in the state. In each locality, voters usually elect a city or town council. Most cities also elect a mayor or city manager. Cities with a population of more than two thousand can draw up and amend their own charters. A charter is a document describing how the community is to be run. Each city has its own set of needs and problems. By having the power to set their own local laws and rules, the citizens of Oklahoma are able to tackle these concerns directly.

Capitol Improvement

Oklahoma's state capitol building is the only one in the world with an oil well drilled beneath it.

★ Mary Fallin, Governor, 2011-2019

Mary Fallin is the first woman to be elected governor of Oklahoma. Prior to her historic election in 2010 and re-election in 2014, Fallin served two terms as a state representative. She was also a two-term lieutenant governor. She graduated from Oklahoma State University.

★ Elizabeth Warren, US Senator, 2012-

Oklahoma City's Elizabeth Warren became the first member of her family to graduate from college. After earning her law degree, Warren worked as a law professor at Harvard and for the US government before her election as US Senator from Massachusetts in 2012. There were calls for her to run for president.

★ Robert Kerr, US Senator, 1949-1963

Robert S. Kerr was one of the most powerful political and business leaders in Oklahoma's history. Born in 1896 near Ada, Kerr served one term as governor and was elected three times as US Senator. He died in his third term. He helped build dams and waterways in the state.

OKLAHOMA ★ ★ ★
YOU CAN MAKE A DIFFERENCE

Contacting Lawmakers

To find contact information for Oklahoma legislators, go to this website:

www.capitolconnect.com/oklahoma/default.aspx

If you are an Oklahoma resident, enter your address information and click "Submit." The page then displays information about your state and federal legislators and how you can contact them.

Battling Bullying

State Representative Lee Denney

Ty Smalley was an eleven-year-old boy from Perkins, Oklahoma. After being bullied in his school for more than two years, Ty fought back for the first time and was suspended by his school for fighting. After he was sent home on May 13, 2010, he went to his room and took his own life.

His father and mother, Kirk and Laura Smalley, decided that they would devote their lives to try and stop bullying in schools. They spoke on television and at hundreds of schools to share Ty's tragic story and educate adults and children about the impact of bullying. In March 2011, Kirk and Laura met privately with President Barack Obama and First Lady Michelle Obama in the White House prior to attending the first ever White House conference on bullying. They also went to the Oklahoma state capital and worked with the state legislature to enact anti-bullying laws.

The Smalley family lives in State Representative Lee Denney's district. In 2011, Rep. Denney co-sponsored a bill to strengthen Oklahoma's laws against bullying in schools. While the first version of the bill was not passed, they kept working. Finally, on June 28, 2013, Governor Mary Fallin signed the School Safety and Bullying Prevention Act into law. The new legislation gave schools a roadmap for how to handle, report, investigate, and punish bullying related incidents.

Energy production has long been an important part of Oklahoma's economy.

Making a Living

For much of Oklahoma's history, the economy has risen and fallen based on demand for the state's mineral and agricultural products. Since the 1990s, however, state officials have made a determined effort to broaden the economy. An increasing number of Oklahomans now work in service industries (where workers provide a service to other people rather than produce things) and in high-tech jobs. Because high-tech jobs require a well-educated workforce, the state is also making efforts to strengthen its educational system. As of 2012, Oklahoma lagged behind the national average in the percentage of adults holding college diplomas and graduate degrees.

Agriculture

Although Oklahoma is known for its oil and natural gas reserves, agriculture is also important to the state. Oklahoma has more than eighty-six thousand farms and ranches, which cover a combined total of about 35 million acres (14.2 million ha). Once, cotton was Oklahoma's chief crop. In recent times, winter wheat has taken its place. In 2013, Oklahoma ranked fifth among all states in wheat production.

Oklahoma is a leading producer in many other categories as well. The state ranks among the national leaders in the production of pecans, peanuts, rye, grain sorghum,

Raising cattle has been big business in Oklahoma for more than a century and a half.

hogs, and cattle and calves. Farms in the Arkansas River valley grow spinach, beans, and carrots. Peach orchards can be found in Eastern and Central Oklahoma, especially around the towns of Porter and Stratford. In the Red River valley, cotton, peanuts, and a range of vegetables are the main crops. Corn and soybeans round out the list of the main foods raised in Oklahoma soil.

The state's most valuable agricultural product is cattle. More than five million cattle and calves graze on Oklahoma's grasslands and fatten in the state's many feedlots. Chickens, hogs, dairy cows, and turkeys are also raised on the state's ranches and farms. Oklahoma's agricultural industry contributed more than $8.5 billion to the state's economy in 2013.

Mining and Energy

Oklahoma's economy in the twentieth century was built on oil. Although the petroleum industry has been less dominant since the 1990s, it is still a major employer statewide. Oil deposits are found in nearly every county in the state. But oil is not the only treasure stored below ground. Natural gas is also found at most of Oklahoma's oil fields. The state has more than eighty thousand producing oil wells and more than forty thousand producing gas wells. Each year, as old wells are retired, hundreds of new wells are drilled. The industry directly contributes more than $26 billion annually to the state economy. Oklahoma ranks fourth among the fifty states in natural gas production and fifth in oil. Pipelines are another source of employment and income. They help move the state's large supply of oil and gas. Workers are needed to build the lines and make sure they are maintained to prevent any possible leaking.

Earthquakes on the Rise

Greater efforts to find and produce oil and natural gas may be coming at great cost. From 1972 through 2007, the National Earthquake Information Center recorded only a small number of earthquakes in Oklahoma each year. Since 2008, however, Oklahoma quakes have grown in strength and number. On November 5, 2011, a quake measuring 5.6 on the Richter scale shook the state. The quake was centered in Central Oklahoma, about 31 miles (50 km) east of Oklahoma City.

In total, more than 2,500 small earthquakes hit Oklahoma from 2008 to 2013, and a recent study suggests that nearly all of them can be linked to the process of drilling for oil and gas. The study, led by Cornell University geophysics professor Katie Keranen, is the latest of many scientific studies showing a probable connection between earthquakes and drilling-related activity across the country.

Drilling may be the cause of an increase in earthquakes in Oklahoma.

At first, some people thought that fracking was causing the earthquakes. Fracking involves pumping water, sand, and other materials under very high pressure into a well. This fractures underground rock and releases oil and natural gas. Now, some scientists believe that putting fracking wastewater in underground wells is more strongly linked to **seismic** activity than fracking itself. Seismic means earthquakes and other shaking of the Earth's crust. They believe that injecting large amounts of water into the ground can change the stress on existing fault lines and cause them to collapse. This results in earthquakes.

The link between earthquakes and disposing of wastewater is not proven.

★ 10 ★ KEY INDUSTRIES

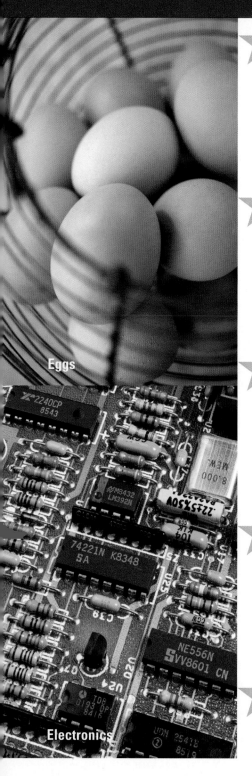

Eggs

Electronics

1. Aviation/Aerospace

With more than three hundred aviation and aerospace firms, Oklahoma now ranks among the top ten states in traditional aerospace employment. Tinker Air Force Base employs the largest group of civilian Air Force personnel in the United States and is Oklahoma's largest single-site employer.

2. Cattle

Beef cattle are the state's top agricultural earner. From raising cattle to processing meat, the cattle industry normally provides many thousands of jobs. Larger cattle operations are usually found in the western part of the state. A severe drought hurt the industry in 2011.

3. Eggs

The poultry industry in Oklahoma supplies the state and the nation with chickens and eggs. Each year, state poultry farmers usually market between 750 million and 800 million eggs. Egg production brings Oklahoma more than $80 million in income annually.

4. Electronics

Electronic equipment ranks high among the state's manufactured products. Tulsa is a center for the production of aerospace equipment. In Oklahoma City, communications equipment is a major product, while aircraft parts are made in Shawnee.

5. Government

This industry sector makes up more than 20 percent of Greater Oklahoma City's employment.

OKLAHOMA ★ ★ ★ ★

6. Iodine

Iodine is vital. The human body depends on it for cell reproduction. It's irreplaceable in medical imaging, and there's a tiny bit in every LCD TV screen. Oklahoma is the nation's sole producer of iodine, with processing plants concentrated in northwest Oklahoma.

7. Oil and Natural Gas

Oklahoma's economy has thrived for years on the strength of its oil and natural gas resources. Technologies to discover and produce oil and natural gas were first tested in Oklahoma.

8. Pecans

The state ranks among US leaders in the production of pecans. The pecan harvest averages about 18 million pounds (8.2 million kg) per year, contributing some $22 million a year, on average, to the state's economy. The tasty nuts are sold to companies around the world.

9. Wheat

Wheat has long been Oklahoma's most important grain crop. The state's industry received a major boost in the late twentieth century with the opening of markets in China. In recent years, wheat production has declined and some Oklahoma farmers have planted crops that bring higher prices.

10. Wind

Wind energy is expanding in Oklahoma, especially in western parts of the state. In 2013, almost 15 percent of Oklahoma's electricity came from wind power. Officials hope the state will become a center for manufacturing turbines and towers.

Oil and Gas

Pecans

Recipe for Praline Pecans

The United States supplies about 80 percent of the world's pecans, and pecans are an important crop for many farmers in Oklahoma. The following recipe uses pecans to make a sweet treat. Be sure to use a heavy saucepan, and work quickly when spooning the pecan mixture onto the wax paper.

What You Need

1½ cups (355 milliliters) granulated sugar

¾ cup (178 mL) firmly packed brown sugar

½ cup (118 mL) butter

½ cup (118 mL) milk

2 tablespoons (29.5 mL) corn syrup

5 cups (1.18 liters) toasted pecan halves

What to Do

- Stir together first five ingredients in a heavy three-quart saucepan.
- Bring to a boil over medium heat, stirring constantly. Boil, stirring constantly, seven to eight minutes or until a candy thermometer registers 234 degrees Fahrenheit (112°C).
- Remove from heat, and vigorously stir in pecans.
- Spoon pecan mixture onto wax paper, spreading in an even layer.
- Let stand twenty minutes or until firm.
- Break praline-coated pecans apart into pieces.
- Store in an airtight container at room temperature up to one week. Freeze in an airtight container or zip-top plastic freezer bag up to one month.

However, Oklahoma is not the only place in America in which there has been an increase in small- to medium-sized earthquakes along with an increase in fracking. A sharp increase in earthquakes in areas where fracking was increased has been seen in Ohio, Arkansas, Texas, and Kansas. The quakes have been small, but some scientists have warned that seismic activity stands to get stronger and more dangerous as fracking increases.

Although oil reigns supreme in the Sooner State, Oklahoma has other valuable mineral resources. Rich beds of coal line parts of northeastern and east-central Oklahoma. The state's uplands provide valuable reserves of sand, gravel, limestone, gypsum, and salt. The sand and gravel are used for concrete and for highway construction and repair. Limestone, often in the form of crushed stone, is found in large quarries in the southwestern part of the state. Gypsum is used for construction and for products such as fertilizer.

Wind Means Energy

Oklahoma generates most of its electricity from natural gas and coal. However, the state has been developing an energy source that does not come from underground—wind. The first modern wind farm in Oklahoma began producing electricity in 2003. With its great expanses of open prairie, Oklahoma offers excellent conditions for additional wind farm construction, especially in western parts of the state.

The prairies are perfect places for Oklahoma's wind farms.

As a resource, Oklahoma's wind ranks number nine in the nation, according to the American Wind Energy Association (AWEA). In 2013, almost 15 percent of the electricity generated in Oklahoma came from wind power, which means the state ranked seventh nationally in terms of how much of the power it uses comes from wind. Oklahoma also ranked fourth among all states for total wind energy generated in 2013.

Several new wind farms are under construction as of 2014, and Governor Mary Fallin and commerce officials hope the state will become a center for manufacturing turbines and towers. The potential for new jobs has led several state technical schools to start programs to train and certify workers in repairing and servicing wind turbines.

Wind energy is largely unregulated in Oklahoma, and local governments have been dealing with disputes between landowners and property developers over wind farm projects.

Manufacturing

Much of the manufacturing in Oklahoma serves the needs of the state's oil and gas drillers, farmers, and military bases. Many factories produce equipment used by the petroleum industry. Products include machine parts, construction equipment, and heating and cooling devices.

Sand Creek in Osage Hills State Park is a popular place to go fishing.

Factories near many of the state's larger cities also turn out high-tech equipment, including motor parts and communication systems used by the US military. Other factories in the state process foods, refine metals, and produce rubber and plastic products. Plants near Tulsa and Oklahoma City assemble cars and trucks and produce equipment for airplanes and spacecraft.

Tourism and Services

Tourism contributes more than $7 billion per year to the Oklahoma economy and provides jobs for about seventy-eight thousand state residents.

Fans are passionate about football at the University of Oklahoma.

State parks located throughout Oklahoma attract more than twelve million visitors per year. Outdoor attractions range from the canyons and ranches of northwestern Oklahoma to the mountains, forests, and scenic waterfalls that mark the southern portion of the state.

Also popular with tourists is the city of Tulsa, sometimes called the "oil capital of the world." Two of the city's major attractions are the Gilcrease Museum, which holds an extensive collection of Native American art and artifacts, and the Philbrook Museum of Art, which has more than 8,500 works in its international collection. The Philbrook is housed in a restored 1920s villa in the heart of the city.

In Oklahoma City, Chesapeake Energy Arena is the home of the Oklahoma City Thunder of the NBA. Tulsa's main sports and performing arts arena is the Bank of Oklahoma (BOK) Center, designed by the celebrated modern architect César Pelli.

The state's major institutions of higher education include the University of Oklahoma, which has its main campus in Norman, and Oklahoma State University, headquartered in Stillwater. In college sports, the University of Oklahoma Sooners have long been a football powerhouse.

Tourism, education, and the health care industry are major sources of employment for workers in the service sector of Oklahoma's economy. Other service employees work in department stores and supermarkets, as well as in restaurants and hotels. Some provide fellow Oklahomans with cars, insurance, legal advice, and new homes. Most service jobs are found in or near Oklahoma's major urban areas. These jobs make up an important part of the state's "new economy" for the twenty-first century.

OKLAHOMA
STATE MAP

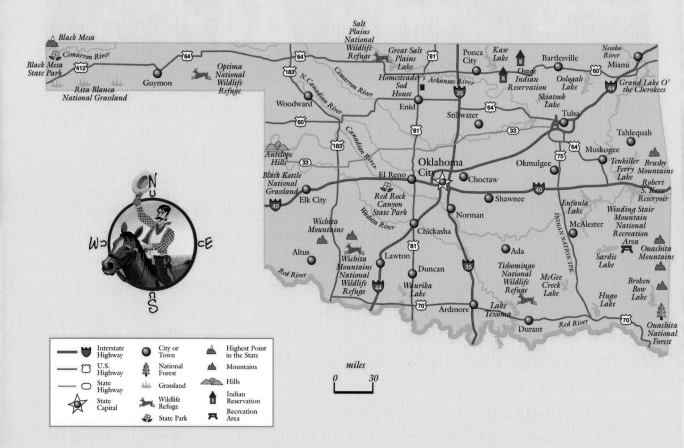

Black Mesa
Cimarron River
Black Mesa State Park
Rita Blanca National Grassland
Guymon
Optima National Wildlife Refuge
Salt Plains National Wildlife Refuge
Great Salt Plains Lake
Ponca City
Kaw Lake
Bartlesville
Neosho River
Miami
412
64
64
183
N. Canadian River
Cimarron River
Homesteader's Sod House
Arkansas River
Osage Indian Reservation
Oologah Lake
Skiatook Lake
60
Grand Lake O' the Cherokees
81
35
Woodward
Enid
Stillwater
64
Tulsa
44
Tahlequah
60
Canadian River
81
33
75
64
Muskogee
183
Antelope Hills
33
Black Kettle National Grassland
El Reno
Oklahoma City
Choctaw
Okmulgee
Tenkiller Ferry Lake
Brushy Mountains
Robert S. Kerr Reservoir
40
Elk City
Red Rock Canyon State Park
Norman
Shawnee
40
Eufaula Lake
McAlester
Winding Stair Mountain National Recreation Area
Ouachita Mountains
Wichita Mountains
Washita River
Chickasha
Ada
INDIAN NATION TPK.
Sardis Lake
Altus
Wichita Mountains National Wildlife Refuge
Lawton
Duncan
81
35
Tishomingo National Wildlife Refuge
McGee Creek Lake
Broken Bow Lake
Waurika Lake
44
70
Ardmore
Lake Texoma
Hugo Lake
70
Ouachita National Forest
Durant
Red River
Red River

Legend

	Interstate Highway		City or Town		Highest Point in the State
Interstate Highway		City or Town		Highest Point in the State	
U.S. Highway		National Forest		Mountains	
State Highway		Grassland		Hills	
State Capital		Wildlife Refuge		Indian Reservation	
		State Park		Recreation Area	

miles
0   30

OKLAHOMA ★ ★ ★ ★
MAP SKILLS

1. **Locate Oklahoma's state capital on the map. What is the closest town or city to the west?**

2. **What three interstate highways meet near Oklahoma City?**

3. **What river forms the southern border of Oklahoma?**

4. **What National Grassland is furthest west in Oklahoma?**

5. **What Native American Reservation is located close to Bartlesville?**

6. **What mountains are closest to the city of Altus?**

7. **Ponca City is located closest to what lake?**

8. **Ouachita National Forest can be found in what corner of the state: Northeast, Northwest, Southeast or Southwest?**

9. **What is the highest point in Oklahoma?**

10. **Woodward is located next to what river?**

Interstate 40 passes through Oklahoma City.

WEST
INTERSTATE
40

Black Mesa

10. N. Canadian River
9. Black Mesa
8. Southeast
7. Kaw Lake
6. Wichita Mountains
5. Osage Indian Reservation
4. Rita Blanca National Grassland
3. Red River
2. Interstates 35, 40, and 44
1. El Reno

State Flag, Seal, and Song

The Oklahoma flag's blue color is symbolic of a flag carried by Choctaw Native American soldiers during the Civil War. An Osage shield stands in the center of the blue background. The center shield, decorated with eagle feathers, is the traditional battle shield of an Osage Native American warrior. Two symbols of peace—the peace pipe and an olive branch—cover the buffalo hide shield. The word "Oklahoma" appears below the many feathers hanging from the shield. The basic design was officially adopted in 1925, and the word "Oklahoma" was added in 1941.

A white star appears in the center of the state seal. In its center, a settler and a Native American shake hands. They stand for the spirit of peace and cooperation that exists among all the peoples of Oklahoma. On the star's five points are symbols of each of the Five Civilized Tribes brought to the state in the early 1800s. Around the star are forty-five smaller stars. They stand for each of the states that entered the Union before Oklahoma became the forty-sixth state. The seal was adopted in 1907.

The state song is the title song of the hit musical *Oklahoma*. It was the first musical written by the famous team of lyricist Oscar Hammerstein II and composer Richard Rodgers. The musical was performed first on March 31, 1943, and it was adopted by the state legislature as the state song on May 11, 1953.

To read the lyrics, visit: **www.statesymbolsusa.org/Oklahoma/stateSONG.html**

Glossary

artifacts	Something created by humans in a particular time period, usually for a practical purpose.
chuck wagon	A wagon carrying a stove and food for cooking for a group of people (such as cowboys).
convention	A large meeting of people who gather, usually for several days, to talk about their shared work or interests or to make decisions.
drought	A long period of time during which there is little or no rain.
earthquake	A shaking of a part of the Earth's surface that often causes great damage.
gypsum	A soft white or gray mineral used to make plaster, fertilizers, and building materials.
mesas	Flat-topped hills with steep sides.
migrate	To move from one country or place to live or work in another.
natural gas	Gas that is taken from under the ground and used as fuel.
reservations	Areas of land in the United States kept separate as a place for Native Americans to live.
reservoir	A place (like a lake, usually man-made) used to store a large supply of water for people.
seismic	Caused by an earthquake or a vibration of the Earth.
sharecropping	A system where an owner lets a tenant farm his land in exchange for a share of the crops.
terrorist	A person who uses violence to frighten people as a way of reaching a political goal.
tornado	A violent and destructive storm in which powerful winds move around a central point.

More About Oklahoma

BOOKS

Dorman, Robert L. *It Happened in Oklahoma.* Guilford, CT: Globe Pequot Press, 2011.

Galvan, Glenda. *Chikasha Stories, Volume One: Shared Spirit.* Sulphur, OK: Chickasaw Press, 2013.

Golus, Carrie. *Jim Thorpe.* Minneapolis, MN: Twenty-First Century Books, 2008.

Henningfeld, Diane Andrews, ed. *The Oklahoma City Bombing (Perspectives on Modern World History).* Detroit, MI: Greenhaven Press, 2012.

WEBSITES

Encyclopedia of Oklahoma History & Culture

digital.library.okstate.edu/encyclopedia

Official Oklahoma Tourism Site

www.travelok.com

Oklahoma City National Memorial & Museum—Official Website

www.oklahomacitynationalmemorial.org

ABOUT THE AUTHORS

Gerard (Gerry) Boehme was born in New York City, graduated from The Newhouse School at Syracuse University, and is an author, editor, and speaker.

Doug Sanders is a writer living in New York City. He enjoys visiting the Wichita Mountains and the Oklahoma City National Memorial.

Geoffrey M. Horn has written more than fifty books for young people and adults. He lives in Red Bank, New Jersey.

Index

Page numbers in **boldface** are illustrations. Entries in **boldface** are glossary terms.

Index